The Church with the Issue of Blood: A Pattern for Reviving Generations

By Kesean J. Joseph

The Church with the Issue of Blood

A Pattern for Reviving Generations

by

Kesean Joseph

Copyright © 2019

First Edition

Scripture marked (NIV) is taken from THE HOLY BIBLE, NEW INTERNATIONAL VERSION®, NIV® Copyright © 1973, 1978, 1984, 2011 by Biblica, Inc.® Used by permission. All rights reserved worldwide. Scripture taken from the New King James Version. Copyright © 1982 by Thomas Nelson, Inc. Used by permission. All rights reserved Scriptures taken from the King James Version are public domain.

All rights reserved. No part of this publication may be reproduced or transmitted in any form or by any means, electronic or mechanical, including photocopy, recording, or any information storage retrieval system, without permission in writing from the copyright owner.

Acknowledgements

First, I would like to honor the **Lord Jesus Christ** who is not only the head of my life but is my life.

To my Mom and Dad, Yvette and Kevin Joseph: I thank you for your undying support and unconditional love toward me. To my siblings, I love each of you and there's nothing that I wouldn't do for you …. except babysit!

Grandma Joseph, I love you and I thank you for your support, strength and your sweet potato pies!

To my Pastors, Archbishop J. C. and Elder Gloria White: affectionately known as Aunt Mama and Uncle Papa: I thank God for you giving me a solid grounding in Word and truth. Thank you for loving and seeing me as a person and not just for what I can do.

To Apostle Brian Keith Williams: truly a preaching Hero of mine, when Archbishop read this book, he said "This is Brian Keith all the way!" Thank you for your constant impartation and for the many messages that you have preached that completely shifted my thinking. You have truly been an inspiration in studying and analyzing the text.

To Bishop Austin Craig and Lady Hadya Williams and my second family: thank you for teaching me to stretch past my limitations and think outside the box. I thank you so much for all you allowed me to experience through you both.

To Bishop Carl E. Williams Jr.: thank you. I would not be where I am today had you not taken the risk and licensed this 11-year old kid. I gave you my word that I would never forget that or forget to honor you for believing in me when no one else knew my name. I love you!

To Bishop Johnathan Alvarado: my Seminary/theology mentor: thank you for your time invested into this project. You are such a blessing to my life.

To Apostle Bryan Meadows: thank you for sharing your wisdom with me on a consistent basis as a distant mentee. I thank God for the anointing that is on your life.

To my Administrator, Amber: thank you for putting up with me! It's hard to assist an administrator but you do it very well and I thank God for you.

To my mentors and sharpeners: Dr. Brian J. Mosley, Bishop Eric A. McDaniel, Prophet Andre Cook, Dr. Cynthia McInnis, Pastor Dwayne Dawkins, Bishop Zebedee Dowtin and Pastor Jonathan Toogood: Each of you have played a significant role in my ministry formation and I thank you from the bottom of my heart.

To all my family, friends, peers and loved ones: THANK YOU!

Dedication

This book is dedicated to the woman who taught me everything I know. My first Bible school professor, my first musical instructor, my first writing coach, my first intercessor: my sainted Grandmother, *Lillian A. Dominick*. She passed suddenly on November 14, 2018 without warning, but she left a legacy that would outlive her for decades. She NEVER hung up the phone with me without saying "Kesean, guard your anointing. It's the most important thing you've got!" I'm guarding it Nana. I love you eternally and I know that I will see you again. **#ByFaithLillian**

Table of Contents

Foreword	11
Introduction: Why Church?	20
Old School Versus New School	30
The Tale of Two Women	36
The Bleeding Church	47
Interlude: Why Bother?	63
The Dying Church	67
The Funeral Is Cancelled	86
Epilogue: Practical Tips	88

Foreword

I am thrilled to recommend Elder Kesean Joseph's outstanding new penning titled, "The Church with the Issue of Blood: A Pattern for Reviving Generations!" There's an unquestionable gulf between those of my generation (43rd year of preaching) and those who weren't even born, when I started. BUT, THE MILLENIALS' ARE THE REPLACEMENTS. Better yet, THE ADVANCEMENTS. THE ENHANCEMENTS. That doesn't discourage, it definitely should encourage.

In every NOW generation, The Almighty God raises up NEW generals, in the making. Messengers whose heart has been fashioned according to His own holiness. Whose lips have been touched by the fiery-hot coals of the Altar, of His hallowed presence. Whose young soul is seasoned with the saturation of generations. Those whose words contain the wisdom of the ancients and the wittiness and winsomeness of the moderns. This Man of God is one of the brightest, most brilliant minds of our post-modern times. The exposition is simple, yet quite profound and the exegesis is profoundly simple. With prophetic exactitude he points at the problem and provides the solutions. He addresses the questions and adeptly questions what some think are the answers.

Throughout history, God has used chosen vessels, who live what they preach and teach what they live. They move His purpose forward and keep the Church from falling backward. In Mesopotamia, He used Abraham, to leave his comfort zone and lay claim to the land of promise, overcoming the compromise of Chaldea. In Egypt, He used Joseph with the concise gift of interpretation to precisely position a Pharaoh, to survive and enable Abraham's seed to revive and thrive. He thrust Moses into the forefront from the backside of a desert, to speak truth to a Controlling Potentate and Let His People Go! In Babylon He gave Daniel revelation from visions and Michael the Archangel the voice, to bring understanding to those under enemy influence. He honored the consecrated lifestyle of three young men, Hananiah, Azariah, and

Mishael, to establish His resolute standard of righteousness, in a foreign, idolatrous land.

He uses Kesean Joseph in this composite discourse, to discover the divide and uncover the generational collide. After Joshua's death there were Elders. After the Elders', there were Judges. Joshua knew God. The Elders knew "about" God. The next generation didn't know God at all. Joshua was consecrated. The Elders were compromised. The next generation was confused. History repeats itself. This generation of believers, are the "generation of those that seek him." They're also, the generation that knows not the Lord, nor the Works He's done" (Judges 2:10). They err, not knowing the "scriptures, nor the power of God

(Matthew 22:29). But, it's not their fault. It's just the truth anyhow.

Recently, a Senior leader editorialized and categorized millennials of simply wanting to have a compromised "Club Church." He criticized the lights, stage, and production aspect of their services. He called it "worldliness." I vociferously acknowledged that, "entertainment is the spirit of the age", but must assert that Church can be done in a myriad of ways. Millennials do things differently today, because IT'S A NEW DAY! The Church is experiencing REVOLUTION in its' EVOLUTION. Traditions can be traded, especially, vain tradition. Catching men and women is like catching fish, according to the Lord. Sometimes, that requires fresh ideas and bait that's different than the status quo. Methods change, principles don't. Truth is simple, not convoluted. If reaching souls is the motive, it's not compromise or conformity, it's "MODERNITY!" Big difference.

A bleeding church has an internal condition of biting and devouring one another by majoring in minors and minoring in majors. Change is inevitable, not regrettable. Some changes are incredible. New Wine requires New Wineskins. Two things cannot change: CHRIST-CENTEREDNESS and the GOSPEL. The song, "A Mighty Fortress Is Our God", was written by Martin Luther. It's a hymn. A classic. At the time, however, some say it was a well-known PUB tune, the drunks sang. Luther changed the words, kept the tune. People were drawn to listen, by its' familiar sound, but drawn to Christ, because of its' lyrics. He was criticized for this. It was a Master Stroke. To reach Millennials, must be masterful, relational, and intentional. Being Reverential Makes God's Presence Residential. When Christ is preached and worshipped wholeheartedly, the Holy Spirit makes the difference. Truth told, "millennials don't know the old ways, because many of the ELDERS forgot them, themselves."

I WHOLEHEARTEDLY ENDORSE THIS BOOK BECAUSE, as Kesean Joseph points out, a bleeding church has an internal condition of biting and devouring one another. Majoring in minors and minoring in majors gets the Church nowhere, quick, fast, and in a hurry. The author reveals that the Bleeding

Church is a barren, childless one. His critique is accurate, not accusative.

Diagnosis is necessary to have a hopeful prognosis. It would be a misdiagnosis to pretend that although the Church is alive and well, that all is well. Millennials are fertile ground. Today, both millennials and elders must together break up fallow ground that the womb of the Church will become fertile once again. Trans-generational ministry, is transformative. I do not perceive their "freedom" as "compromise." Its' causative and creative. It's A NEW DAY. Some things must be done a NEW WAY! The author is destined to be a MAJOR MOVER AND SHAKER AMONG THE MILLENIALS and has the hopefulness of youth and the heart of the Father. This writing will reach the ear of the elders and just as the young Lord Jesus brought Doctors' to a state of wonderment, so will he. His youth shouldn't and mustn't be despised, nor, should this prophecy. HE IS THE LORD'S ANOINTED. HEAR YE HIM!

Live READY,
Bishop Dr. Brian Keith WIlliams
Apostolic Network of Churches
Floating Church Dock INC.
Orlando, Florida

Introduction: Why Church?

I am passionate about the revival of the local church body, because the local Church has been a vital part of our society for centuries, especially in the black community. The church was the driving force behind the Abolitionist movement, the Civil Rights movement, and the educational advancement of our people. The church continues to be the charity arm of communities through pantries, scholarships, and community programs. One of the reasons people can have a misguided picture of the Church is because, unfortunately, the media seems to only cover the financially excessive and corrupt ministries instead of the many sincere and pure churches.

The statement about hypocrites being in the church can be true in some cases, but I try to avoid using the saying, "There are hypocrites in the club, but you still go." The very fact that we are comparing saints of God to people in the world is a huge problem. The expectations of people who enter the house of God should be different. Instead, I would say, "Where else should they go?" The best place for a hypocrite to be is in church, that is where they are confronted with the truth. Getting angry at a sinner in church is like getting angry at an overweight person at the gym. There's nothing more ridiculous than shaming an overweight person who is trying to get their weight under control, yet, we do it. Likewise, we shame sinners and hypocrites for being in the very place they're supposed to be to get help. Furthermore, the moment we accuse someone of being a hypocrite, we are judging them just like we claim they are judging us. Make sure that you are not guilty of the same, otherwise, you are a hypocrite too. Do you see how easily that word can be thrown around?

The other problem with referring to someone as a hypocrite is that this label comes from unrealistic and unfair expectations. I sincerely apologize if Christians in your life have created a perception that our faith is one of spotless perfection. Christianity is a walk of forgiveness, redemption, and grace. The more we receive God's forgiveness and grace, the stronger we grow in righteousness. However, we are just as human as everyone else. It seems that anytime a believer falls or makes a mistake, hypocrite becomes the buzzword. Just because a person falls short does not mean that they are a hypocrite. Hypocrisy is not failure, it is acting or faking. It's easy to not fail at living a righteous life when you don't even try. The house of God should be a place of people working out their soul salvation with fear and trembling.[1]

Jesus Christ established the church and promised us that the gates of hell will not prevail against it.[2] We are not just saved to an individual faith. We are saved into a community of believers: the body of Christ. The very nature of our faith is communal and cooperative. Our faith is relational. Here are some biblical reasons for the public assembly of the local church:

---

[1] Philippians 2:12
[2] Matthew 16:18

To obey the Bible	Hebrews 10:25, Acts 2:42
To learn dependence on one another	1 Corinthians 12:13-26
To be part of the family through salvation	Romans 8:16 & 29, Galatians 6:10
To experience fivefold gifts	Ephesians 4:11-16
To benefit the whole body	1 Corinthians 12:13-26, 14:1-4
To confess and be held accountable by each other	James 5:16
To exercise the power of agreement	Matthew 18:19-20
To rehearse the joy of	Revelation 7:9

assembling in Heaven	
To see the beauty of unity	Psalm 117:1-2

The local church has served as a bedrock for the community for centuries. It has cultivated many talented artists, both secular and religious. It has provided a sense of family for those who didn't have one or were rejected by their own. Some have been wounded by the church, but not everyone. There are some of us that have found a safe place and refuge in our local churches. For many, the Pastor was the only father-figure they had. I have watched my Pastors pay bills from their own pockets, testify in court, and minister to people on multiple occasions. There is power in the local church. I am reminded of early church Father Cyprian who once said, "He does not have God as a Father, who does not have the church as a mother."[3]

Why This Book?

I am a churchman. I am a fourth generation Pentecostal. My great-grandparents were founding members of the First Church of God in Christ under the leadership of Bishop Frank Clemmons, a great Pentecostal pioneer. My great Uncle, Bishop Carl Williams Sr, founded and pastored the Institutional Church of God in Christ International for over 50 years. My current Pastor and Uncle, Archbishop J.C.

---

[3] Clarke, Graeme W., and Graeme Wilber Clarke, eds. *The Letters of St. Cyprian of Carthage* (Mahwah, NJ, Paulist Press, 1984), 33.

White, is the writer of many of the church choir standards of today.

I was born and raised in the Church. Growing up, I was the only one in my household that attended church. I love the church and all it has to offer. I love the Church and the people of the church, flaws and all. Although I have had hard times, I could never see myself abandoning my church. I say this to make it clear that this is NOT a writing to divide the Church, to stir strife, or to speak against Christ's holy body. This book is meant to be one of answers and solutions.

I believe the Lord has called me to be a generational bridge within His church. Because I was raised by my maternal grandmother in church, I have a unique perspective of both sides of the generational coin. I can remember my church holding onto devotional services. I also remember the rise of modern praise and worship. I know the traditional hymns and the modern worship songs. I like wearing suits and vestments, but I also enjoy dressing down sometimes too. I believe these elements of the church and of our Christian lives don't have to be at war with each other. I believe that we can come together and do the work of the ministry together.

This book is not necessarily to address problems in the body of the church at large, although it may. I try not to do that to avoid generalizing. As I speak hypothetically of local churches, you will find it often mirrors the body as a whole. I believe this writing will help those in the local Church who find themselves in the middle of the war of generations—those who stand between the old school versus the new school. This writing is for those who love devotional songs and still love the guitar-driven ballads of our day. This is for those who pastor a historic church that is losing its members or has very few to begin with. I dedicate this writing to those who are in charge of the youth in their Church or organization and are searching for answers to the growth of their ministry. I pray that this book gives you answers.

Old School Versus New School

The last verse of Malachi, the last book of the Old Testament says, "**And he will turn The hearts of the fathers to the children, And the hearts of the children to their fathers, Lest I come and strike the earth with a curse (Malachi 3:6, NKJV)."**

This scripture comes after 612 laws of Moses, 150 psalms, and 17 prophetic writings about sin, righteousness, bondage, liberty, theology, and morality. One may assume that the way God would close the entire Old Testament canon would be with a reference to the law, sacrifice, or one of the many other themes present in the Old Testament. Yet God devotes his final instruction to His people on intergenerational relationships.

In context, Malachi is prophesying concerning the Day of the Lord. This was considered a major event in the Old Covenant prophecy. This event will be marked by the coming of the Messiah to bring righteousness to the earth. After the prophet Malachi gives rebukes in the first few chapters, he closes with words of exhortation and encouragement to those who are faithful to the Lord amongst great sin and falling away. Verse 5 states that God will send the Prophet Elijah before the coming of the Lord. To avoid taking a theological position about the end times, we will just declare this represents powerful prophetic ministry that precedes the coming of the Lord. Prophet Malachi then says that prophetic ministry will turn the hearts of generations to one another. The consequences for generational division are striking, resulting in God striking the land with utter destruction.

On the flipside, we see from scripture that great things happen when generations come together! For example, in Joel 2:28 (NKJV), the Prophet says that God will "pour out his spirit on all flesh." He then says, "the sons and daughters shall prophesy, your old men shall dream dreams and your young men shall see visions." Joel paints revival as an intergenerational explosion!

This shows us that God desires there to be a strong connection between the old and the young, and naturally, the enemy would fight the body of Christ in that very place. The last few years in the church can be best described as a cold war between the generations. My experience has allowed me to see this the most in the charismatic churches, but research shows that the conflict can also be seen in other denominations as well. The Christian culture is warring over things such as what to wear, what to sing, and preaching and teaching styles and has also been the subject of viral videos, messages, hashtags and more.

    The Church is an institution built on relationships and it suffers when the relationships between its members are on the rocks. The enemy has divided the Church by age and has influenced this feuding between the seasoned saints and the millennials and vice versa. In my experience, the elder generations say millennials are unteachable and are "know-it-all's." The millennials say the older people are stubborn and ignorant. The elder generation seems to be heavily focused on tradition and the way things used to be. Some millennials have been so wounded by the traditions of men that they throw out the baby with the bathwater, and the bathtub. Some millennials have suffered spiritual manipulation, abuse, and bad dogma at the hands of the elder generations. And in some cases, the elder generations have suffered disrespect, neglect, or are made to feel their labor was for naught because of ignorance. There are nuances, shades of gray and exceptions within both groups. I have encountered millennials who are traditional and want churches to revert to the 1950s and 1960s. I have also observed older generations who say they never even knew Jesus for themselves until now and the old church was the worst experience of their lives. While we are feuding, we are missing opportunities for impartation from the older saints and execution from the younger.

The Tale of Two Women

Now when Jesus had crossed over again by boat to the other side, a great multitude gathered to Him; and He was by the sea. And behold, one of the rulers of the synagogue came, Jairus by name. And when he saw Him, he fell at His feet and begged Him earnestly, saying, 'My little daughter lies at the point of death. Come and lay Your hands on her, that she may be healed, and she will live.' So *Jesus* went with him, and a great multitude followed Him and thronged Him.

Now a certain woman had a flow of blood for twelve years, and had suffered many things from many physicians. She

had spent all that she had and was no better, but rather grew worse. When she heard about Jesus, she came
behind *Him* in the crowd and touched His garment. For she said, 'If only I may touch His clothes, I shall be made well.' Immediately the fountain of her blood was dried up, and she felt in *her* body that she was healed of
the affliction. And Jesus, immediately knowing in Himself that power had gone out of Him, turned around in the crowd and said, 'Who touched My clothes?' But His disciples said to Him, 'You see the multitude thronging You, and You say, 'Who touched Me?' And He looked around to see her who had done this thing. But the woman, fearing

and trembling, knowing what had happened to her, came and fell down before Him and told Him the whole truth. And He said to her, 'Daughter, your faith has made you well. Go in peace, and be healed of your affliction.'

While He was still speaking, *some* came from the ruler of the synagogue's *house* who said, 'Your daughter is dead. Why trouble the Teacher any further?' As soon as Jesus heard the word that was spoken, He said to the ruler of the synagogue, "Do not be afraid; only believe." And He permitted no one to follow Him except Peter, James, and John the brother of

James. Then He came to the house of the ruler of the synagogue, and saw a tumult and those who wept and wailed loudly. When He came in, He said to them, 'Why make this commotion and weep? The child is not dead, but sleeping.' And they ridiculed Him. But when He had put them all outside, He took the father and the mother of the child, and those *who were* with Him, and entered where the child was lying. Then He took the child by the hand, and said to her, 'Talitha, cumi,' which is translated, 'Little girl, I say to you, arise.' Immediately the girl arose and walked, for she was twelve years *of age*. And they were overcome with great amazement. But He commanded them strictly that no one should know it, and said that *something* should be given her to eat.

– Mark 5:25-43, NKJV

Now, compared to the passages from Malachi and Joel, the story I chose for the main topic of this book is different. In Mark chapter 5, Jesus has just come off the boat from the Gadarenes. Upon his arrival, a large crowd surrounds Him and follows Him. At the same time, a synagogue leader by the name of Jairus notifies Jesus that his daughter is near death. There is no explanation of what the disease is or why she has it. Jesus is simply told that this 12-year-old girl is dying. Imagine that, she hasn't even begun to live her life and there she is, standing at death's door. Oh, but our Lord

Jesus consents to come and heal her. On His way there, with Jairus leading the way through the pressing crowd, a woman joins the press. Although she looks normal on the outside, she has an issue of blood for 12 years. She has gone from doctor to doctor trying to get some sort of relief from the disease. This nameless woman had to be isolated because of her condition. But on this day, she thought, "If I can but touch the Hem, I will be made whole." See the full story in Mark 5:21-43.

    Within the stories of the woman with the issue of blood and of Jairus' daughter may be the last place one would look for a message about reviving generations. But that is exactly what I see there! As I wish to point out here, Mark was also notorious for pointing out the curious events in Jesus' ministry. In this story, we see two women, one young and one old—one dying quickly, and another dying slowly, both needing a touch from the Master.

Often, this text is used to talk about our "issues" or is turned into a "fix-it" message, as I would call it. This seems to be the trend of our preaching in today's time. Yet, this single-minded approach is part of the problem.

Once we understand that God has constructed us as a body, and not as individuals, we can begin to view our Christian lives differently. You see, Satan isn't just after you, he's after the entire body of Christ. He truly doesn't care about us individually; his agenda is to destroy the Kingdom of God. You and I are a small part of a much larger war.

Unfortunately, while many of us are going about proclaiming our ambitions and desires, and shouting about God "turning it around," the Church, as a body, is suffering. When I speak of the "Church," I speak of the local institution as Christ spoke of the seven churches in Revelation chapters 1-3.

Now before you say, "There's nothing wrong with my Church, we're growing just fine," take into account that we exist as a body. Ultimately, as one church suffers, we all suffer because we are all part of the body of Christ. Although there are churches that are growing, the number of people who "love God but don't love church" is growing rapidly also.[4] Many

---

[4] "Meet Those Who 'Love Jesus But Not the Church,'" Barna Group, accessed December 12, 2018, https://www.barna.com/research/meet-love-jesus-not-church

millennials are not identifying with any religion at all and don't consider faith to be important, according to that same research article.

At this point, I imagine you're wondering, "What does that have to do with the woman with the issue of blood and Jairus' daughter?" Let me explain. In the Scripture, women are often used as types or symbols of the church. Look at some of these examples from Scripture:

- **Paul uses an analogy of law (Judaism) and grace (Church) through Hagar and Sarah (Galatians 3).**
- **Paul calls the Church the bride of Christ (2 Cor. 11:1-2).**
- **Paul relates a man's wife to Christ's Church (Ephesians 5:25).**

- **John depicts the Church as the Bride (Revelation 21).**
- **The Old Testament often refers to Israel and Zion with female pronouns (Isaiah 4:5).**

There is something so powerful about the feminine nature that God chose to use them to typify the Church or the collective body in Scripture. There are two women in this story of two different ages. I am likening these women to two different generations of church congregations.

I have taken the allegorical liberty to designate the older churches and saints as the "Bleeding Church" or the woman with the issue of blood. In my estimation, millennials and younger churches are, the "Dying Church" or Jairus' daughter.

The woman with the issue of blood suffered for 12 years. Jairus' daughter was 12 years old when she became sick unto death. They both were desperately in need of divine intervention. We should never think that someone is too young or too old to be attacked by the enemy. Satan wants to destroy us all. Yet, with this story, Christ gave us a pattern on how to revive generations. It is not my intention to discourage you with the terms "Bleeding Church" and "Dying Church," but to show you that Christ can heal them both!

The Bleeding Church

The Older Generation

Let me begin by clarifying what I mean by the older generations. The older generations would consist of Baby Boomers, Generation X, and in the rare case, the Builders. The following is a typical breakdown of each generation by age:

- The Builders: 1920 and 1946
- The Baby Boomers: 1946-1964
- Generation X: 1965-1979

The source of conflict can be best understood when we understand the culture of those ages. The Builders are called such because they "built" the foundation of much of our American society after World War II. It is sometimes called the "Greatest Generation." They are those who built many of society's longest standing institutions, including the churches. These are those who purchased pews in the church and mortgaged their homes to pay for the church. They sacrificed their last dollar to support the body of Christ. These were heavily value- and duty-centered people. The Baby Boomers followed close behind and continued some of the same practices.

    It seems that Generation X often felt the brunt of the sacrifices made by the Builders and the Boomers and thus they developed a negative perception of church and ministry as a grueling and draining place. Generation X was the first to emphasize a balance of work and other areas of life. Church became included in work and was thus made to be balanced with their personal life just like their jobs.

The characteristics of this generation are duty-centered function, hard work, and emphasis on values over understanding and intellect. Pastor Jay Patrick writes, "[Generation X] were taught to produce rather than to reason and to focus on reality rather than logic…they were raised to do…The preaching of Generation X was infused with endurance, perseverance, overcoming, staying the course and keeping your hands to the plow."[5]

This generation's emphasis on duty rather than reason would create conflict between them and Generation Y (millennials). I

---

[5] Jay Patrick, *The Millennial Manual* (Huntsville, AL: Keen Vision Publishing, 2017), 13 & 17.

am of the opinion that the Builders Generation had a mixture of duty and reason. In fact, their knowledge of the reason is what caused them to build. Unfortunately, the Builders Generation is quickly disappearing, as we go further into the 21st Century, and they are taking their wisdom with them.

The Church with the Issue of Blood

Although I am speaking about older churches, newer churches can be Bleeding Churches as well. My emphasis is more on mentality than age, although the two can be intertwined. Being considered an "old church" is not based on the age of attendees, but on the age of their mentality. I know many older saints who are open-minded and forward-focused. I also know many millennials who have very dated mindsets.

To understand why I call it the Bleeding Church we must examine the disease of the woman with the issue of blood. Scholars believe that the issue of blood was a disease that resulted in a continual menstrual cycle for 12 years. Yes, you read that correctly, 12 years. It is basic scientific fact that a woman's cycle is essential to her reproductive abilities. Thus, if a woman constantly bleeds, she will be unable to bear children. Even when she does conceive, her body will unintentionally abort the seed she's carrying within a short amount of time. The only way that she can have children is to adopt someone else's children.

Symptom #1: No New Births

One of the symptoms of a Bleeding Church is that it is unable to reproduce. There are fewer and fewer new converts and new "births" in her churches. And it seems that whenever they do finally conceive or get someone to join the church, they leave soon after joining. The altar may be flooded at a funeral, but the pews are soon empty again. Bleeding Churches are unable to retain souls within their spiritual womb. As soon as a new soul comes within their womb, they miscarry and ultimately lose them. Sometimes these souls go to another ministry and sometimes they go nowhere at all.

This feminine process is a cleaning process to prepare for a new baby. But a miscarriage is a sign of malfunction when the body is trying to clean out what should be retained and nurtured. Before a soul can be cleaned, it must be retained within the nurturing place of the church.

Symptom #2: Survival by Adoption

Another symptom of a Bleeding Church is that their attendance survives only by adoption. You may think that this can't be true, because there are still megachurches around. And while there are many that do exist, the population of most of the "successful" churches' consists of people that migrated from another ministry. Thom Rainer, a church researcher, stated that "a few churches are getting bigger at the expense of smaller churches…The old barrier that held people in specific churches—family connections, denominational loyalty, and loyalty to a specific congregation—are no longer barriers today. People move with great freedom from church to church.[6]"

If one compares the number of new converts with average church attendance, the numbers do not add up. There is a growing number of people who "love Jesus but not church." They practice an individually customized form of Christian faith privately and don't attend a local body. Therefore, many of the ministries survive off of "adopting" members from another local church. In Brooklyn, we call it "member swapping."

Symptom #3: Loss of Life and Vitality

---

[6] "Five Reasons Why Churches Are Dying and Declining Faster Today," Thom Rainer, accessed December 14, 2018, https://thomrainer.com/2016/09/five-reasons-churches-dying-declining-faster-today/

Blood gives life to your body. The youth are the life of the church. As stated above, many of them are leaving family churches and historic churches in favor of newer, larger, more modern, contemporary churches. Therefore, many of the historic churches consist of older members and people loyal to the tradition of faithfulness to one ministry. With the departure of youth, there is often a loss of creativity, life, and vibrancy that they bring.

It pains me to see many of our landmark churches now empty, silent, and cold. While they are still absolutely beautiful on the outside, they lack life and newness on the inside. The church membership does not reflect the community around them. Thus, many of them close down or sell their property. In some cases, those that remain have services that praise their traditions, memorials, and ancestors instead of the Holy Spirit and the God of our fathers.

Touch the Hem, Be Made Whole

Remedy #1: Escape the Traditions of Men

According to the teaching of the Law, when a woman was on her monthly cycle, she could not leave her home.[7] According to the Pharisees interpretation of the law, this woman should have stayed in the house.

However, the problem for this woman wasn't just a monthly cycle! This was a disease that persisted for 12 years. Now, this is a picture of a particular problem that is too often

---

[7] Leviticus 15:19

present in our churches today. The trouble with unbridled devotion to rules and protocol is that it often doesn't leave room for humanity, frailty, and the unexpected battles with which the enemy tends to engage us. Life rarely throws us black and white, cookie cutter problems.

Now let me be abundantly clear, there is nothing wrong with protocol, but the church should never place protocol above people. Unfortunately, in too many instances, Bleeding Churches have elevated traditions and rules over the spiritual health of the people they are called to serve.[8] The result is spiritual death because "the letter kills" (2 Corinthians 3:6). If the woman with the issue of blood had followed the Pharisees

---

[8] Now, the critique I offer is not of Biblical doctrine, but rather of idiosyncratic traditions or the stuff we made up.

interpretation of the law and not broke with tradition, she would have bled to death in isolation. Bleeding Churches rarely lack rules, beautiful vestments, and titles, but they lack people. As the church, our first ministry is to souls. The Pharisees made this mistake of esteeming beautiful traditions over broken people. In Matthew 23:27, Jesus called them whitewashed tombs—beautiful on the outside but on the inside, full of the bones of the dead. They had neglected the weightier matters of the law such as love, mercy, and justice in exchange for formalism. As a result, their beautiful buildings became full of dead people on the inside.

Again, there is *nothing* wrong with following protocol and doing things in an orderly manner. I believe in structure wholeheartedly. A disorderly church is a dangerous church. But when it comes down to it, we must know when to lay protocols aside and pursue the Spirit of the law Who is Christ (2 Corinthians 3:17). We don't serve a rigid, cookie cutter Savior. Unique problems call for a personal, living Savior who can reach us by name and by situation, no matter where we are.

The Spirit of the Lord is able to make dead men live and to heal all bleeding within and without.

Remedy #2: Escape Religious Pride

The moment one breaks past the traditions of men, one will gain access to the hem of his garment. To access the hem, the woman had to be in a very humble position, either on her knees or crawling. This attitude of humility is important, not only for seasoned saints, but also for people who have been in church their entire life, including myself. Sometimes, when we serve for a long time, we can become too familiar, passive, and desensitized with the things of the Lord. We become altar workers, preachers, worship leaders, and more, but we must NEVER lose our 'seek.' Seek meaning our passion or desire for the Lord. Sometimes it takes bleeding, personally and corporately, for us to truly seek God. I pray that I never become numbed to the awesomeness of the presence and power of the Lord. Thank God for the vestments, but I'm content with the hem of His garment. You can't touch a hem while standing up with your head in the sky. You have to come down as in humility. We should never forget how to come to the altar and humble ourselves to seek the Lord.

Remedy #3: Testify!

We would have never known this woman's miracle if she had not told it to the disciples and to the Lord Jesus. I will discuss this again later in the book, but transparency is the key to reaching the hearts of men. This is a generation of stories, anecdotes, and experiences. Testimonies bring the Bible to life and remind people of the nearness of God. When God transforms your ministry, tell others about it. Don't let religious pride keep you silent. Tell how the Lord stopped the bleeding and restored your local body. This will not only bless other parishioners, but

Pastors and leaders as well. Sharing how you overcame the bleeding will influence other leaders to implement strategies to transform their ministry as well.

Interlude: Why Bother?

"While Jesus was still speaking, some people came from the house of Jairus, the synagogue leader. "Your daughter is dead," they said. '<u>Why bother</u> the teacher anymore?'"

– Mark 5:35, NIV

This question was posed to Jairus while Jesus was still ministering to the woman with the issue of blood. I'd imagine there was great excitement and joy that this woman, the Bleeding Church, was healed. Amidst the joy, notification comes that Jairus' daughter, the next generation, is now dead. The next question is a vital one: "*Why bother* the teacher anymore?"

If you want to see revival and wonders in the next generation and see them saved and filled with the Holy Ghost, you must push past the place called *"why bother?"* (Thank you for this, Bishop Eric McDaniel.)

Every senior pastor, youth pastor, evangelist, teacher, preacher, worship leader, director, and so on has been to the place called "why bother?"

- Why bother coming to the church?
- Why bother investing my time and money into so few people?
- Why bother preaching when they probably won't apply it or listen?
- Why bother when they will probably leave church when they get older?

- Why bother taking time with them when they will probably stab me in the back and forget my work later?

Indifference is the enemy to deliverance and revival. In verse 36, Jesus' response to Jairus gives the answer to all of these questions: "Don't be afraid. Only believe." The next time someone asks you, "Why bother?" say, "Because I believe God!" If you can push past indifference, passivity, and frustration, Jesus will come to your house! Your ability to resist indifference is a test to your dedication to the cause of Christ. God wants to know how serious you are about seeing this generation saved. We press, we labor, we preach, and we pray because "we believe God."

I believe that Jairus symbolizes what we as leaders need to become in order to bring revival to our generations. Jairus was a synagogue ruler. He had an understanding of the law, customs, and traditions of the Jewish faith. Yet he also had a young daughter that needed immediate healing from Jesus. He did not stop Jesus from ministering to the bleeding church but refused to settle for the death of the next generation. I believe God will greatly use those who understand the traditional way yet are still able to hear the cries of the next generation in need of great deliverance. May God raise up people with an evangelistic attitude like Jairus who know where to find Jesus and know who to bring Him to.

The Dying Church

Who Are the Millennials?

Before going further, I want to give a little background on millennials. "Millennial" is not an "age club" like teenagers. It is based on the year one was born. When someone turns 16, they don't become a millennial. As of now, they would be considered Generation Z. Millennials are those of us born between 1980-1996, some say 1999. This age group constitutes the young adults and the adult population in society, as well as in the church. However, millennials' perception of life in general is different than the other generations before it.

Millennials are more opinionated, introverted, and investigative compared to the other generations. They are called "Generation Why" because they are more inquisitive. They don't just follow blindly; they want to know the logical reason behind what they are doing. The trend of society is toward personalization and convenience. Technology, information and services are being customized toward us, our wants and our needs. Almost everything is created for our convenience. This has caused some sociologists to label millennials as the most narcissistic and entitled generation.

These traits have proven controversial and often cause millennials to be scrutinized by the older generations, yet the technology available to this generation contributes to their desire to know and understand the "why" of what they do. Many traditional businesses and institutions have declined significantly in the day of the Millennials and Generation Z, such as: taxi services, department stores, cable television companies, and even chain restaurants. It is only natural that the institution of the church would also suffer as a result of the changing times and the attitudes of millennials.

My fellow millennials and Generation Z would constitute what I call the "Dying Church," according to the story of Jairus' daughter. I'm not insinuating that one is worse than the other, because technically, both the young girl and the older woman were dying. The story does not give the girl a name nor is much said of her disease, just that she is dying. I refrain from using the term "dead church" in my correlation because Jesus never referred to Jairus' daughter as "dead." He acknowledged that she was sick, but He did not acknowledge her death. All is not lost for this generation, for there is still resurrection power in Christ.

Unfortunately, as a whole, American churches are in a critical state. There is spiritual death due to declining morals, increased schisms, and emphasis on personality over principles. There is also physical death due to increased police brutality against minorities, increased suicide and suicidal attempts, increased depression and subsequent suicides of pastors, and a terrifying amount of mass shootings in our schools and public areas. With all the freedoms given to this generation, the love of many still waxes cold (Matthew 24:12).

There are many causes of inward death in the Bible:

- Lack of true vision or prophetic revelation – Proverbs 29:18
- Lack of knowledge – Hosea 4:6
- Pleasure-driven behavior – 1 Timothy 5:6
- Religion without a living relationship with Christ – Revelation 3:1-2

All of these can be argued as increasingly present amongst my generation. But thank God, we serve Jesus Christ who is the Resurrection and the Life.

Interestingly enough, there are no details of symptoms given about the young girl as there are with the woman with the issue of blood, only solutions. I think that detail is significant. First, I believe it speaks to the mysterious nature of what plagues our youth. Second, it's a blessing because we do more than enough complaining, critiquing, and criticizing of millennials. Millennials are constantly the subject of panels, articles, viral videos, and countless sermons. The Gospel writers do not discuss the young girl's issues, only how Jesus healed her. Therefore, instead of talking about the symptoms of the generation, I will talk about how Jesus raised her up in Mark 5.

Remedy #1: House Call

The Woman with the issue of blood came to Jesus herself, but when it came to the young girl, Jesus went to her. Gone are the days when people come to church every

Sunday because it's the right thing to do. Gone are the days when people turn to faith as an answer to their problems. The seasoned people know how to seek God because it was taught to many of them. But now we have a generation that is unable to do so. The young girl did not come to Jesus herself, but it was not out of rebellion that she didn't come to Him. She couldn't come to Jesus because she was confined to her bed and later, dead.

Much of this generation is not just lost, they're spiritually dead. Therefore, the next great move of God will be on those who, like Jairus, will get Jesus and bring him to the next generation. We cannot afford to stay in the house anymore. We must not continue preaching to the choir in the hopes that someone will stumble in. We must bring the power to wherever they are: the prisons, the schools, the college campuses, and the hospitals. If the millennials can't or won't come to God, we must bring Jesus to them! One of the reasons that the modern church is dying is because it seems we have many Apostles and Prophets, but few Evangelists. I don't just mean those that come and run revivals for our ministries, but I mean those that have a passion for lost souls and that can develop creative methods of outreach. It is through evangelism that the house of God is made full.

Remedy #2: Crash the Pity Party

When Jesus and Jairus come to where the girl lay, the Scripture states there is a great tumult (Mark 5:38). In ancient Jewish culture, the tumult was a group of people hired to come mourn a dead person. Yes, you read that correctly. They were *hired* to mourn a person, whether they knew them or not. These were not silent tears or muzzled cries, these people were wailing at the top of their lungs. Jesus comes in and says, "Why are you making this commotion and weep. The child is not dead but sleeping" (Mark 5:39, NKJV).

    The Scripture says that they quickly go from wailing to laughing hysterically. Isn't that something interesting? This text teaches me that some people only like you when you're broken and in a dysfunctional place. Some people want attention, not a solution. Therefore, when a solution comes, they flat out reject it. Beware of those who dwell in negativity and try to find an issue with everything. If these people really cared for this young girl, they would have jumped at any opportunity for hope.

Millennials are surrounded by wailers, both within and without our generation. Wailers are people that love to point out the issue yet refuse to develop a solution. I am utterly convinced that many people make a living off of those going in circles around the problem; finding a solution would put them out of business. Many counselors, politicians, and other public figures are wailers. A dear friend of mine would say, "A fool can identify a problem. The genius is one who develops a solution."

This room was definitely full of people. Yet, Jesus put every wailer out! Jesus was never impressed with crowds. The last few years of church history are marked by what

Christian researchers call "The Church Growth Movement." Since the Charismatic Revival of the 1960s, there has been an explosion of ministries into megachurches. Thus, the prevailing focus has been on growing and multiplying memberships. We often mark a successful church by how many members they have, how large the building is, social media followership, and so on.

Yet with the increase of megachurches, there has been a significant decline in morality, biblical doctrines, and community. We must be careful to remember that the church is not the building, it is the people. True church growth is when you grow people, not just increase numbers. We must see them as God's people, not just another seat. That being said, you cannot be afraid of losing some people and becoming "small." We must not be afraid to excuse people that are in the way of the revival. Before we see revival, we will see the dismissal of naysayers, backbiters, gossipers, and those that stir discord among us. These are the people that hinder others within the church from getting what they need from the Lord. These are those who often push millennials away from the church. It's time out for playing church, we need Jesus too much.

Remedy #3: The First Small Group

The number of people in the room has now gone from many to only Peter, James, John, Jairus, Mrs. Jairus, Jesus, and a dead girl. This does not look like success in the modern leader's eyes. This looks like a serious loss. Yet God does his best work with what we considered little. God is a God of seed. He can do more with your little than He can with your much. As Dr. Brian Mosley once said, "Four of a kind beats a full house." With Christ, there's more power in agreement than in quantity. God would rather have two or three gathered together in His name, than an entire city who does not believe (such as the city of Nazareth).

The next key to revival is very practical: small groups. The strongest Christians don't grow from attending the Sunday morning service, they grow during the week. They grow through Bible studies and personal conversations. Statistics show that millennials strongly prefer smaller groups and those that are the most Biblically-grounded Christians attend small group discussions. Jesus was truly on to something! At my church, I have young people who come to my small group that wouldn't come on Sunday mornings.

Remedy #4: Deliverance Is a Contact Sport

Traditional Judaic law had strict rules about Rabbis touching dead things or people. Death, bacteria, and disease was a mysterious thing and therefore a corpse was considered unclean. The coming of the Lord Jesus Christ changed many of the old paradigms and traditions. He was not afraid of her uncleanness; he was not afraid to touch her. We as believers cannot be afraid to touch the unclean. We may not touch unclean things, but we do touch unclean people! We don't participate in their sin, but we care for their soul. Now, in Christ, instead of us becoming unclean, they catch our cleanness. Look at Job 22:30 (NKJV), "He will *even* deliver one who is not innocent; Yes, he will be delivered by the purity of your hands."

The touch is not only a point of contact, but also a sign of intimacy and personal relationship. Deliverance is a contact sport! It requires love and compassion for the person in need. Millennials and Generation Z are relationship-driven people. We are those who grew up into social media, which is all about relationships. If you want to see revival in the generation of the millennials, you cannot just preach at them. You can't talk to them from the other side of the room. Nor should you only touch them to chastise them. Love, mentorship, and transparency are all keys to winning the souls of these younger generations for Christ. The preachers that millennials gravitate toward thrive off of being personal. They tell many stories, share failures and successes, and maintain transparency. It is the touch of Jesus that raises the young girl up. It will be the personal touch of the Body of Christ that will resurrect the Dying Church.

Remedy #5: Eat!

Not only did Jesus give the girl a personal touch, but He gave her a Word also, "Talitha cumi," which means, "Little girl, arise." The girl arises and begins to walk. Everyone is in astonishment that she is mobile again. After Jesus charges them to tell no one, He commands that she be given something to eat. Luke actually records that Jesus requested she be given some meat (Luke 8:55).

Millennials, if you want to continue to function and grow in God, you MUST eat! I don't mean natural food, but the Word of God. I am afraid that many in the millennial generation (my generation) are spiritually malnourished. We are feasting on the milk of the Word, things that we should consume as new converts. We cannot build our faith on quips, clichés, and catchy sayings. That is building on the wrong foundation, and when the trials do come, the foundation will swiftly crumble. Praise breaks and high worship are celebrations of what we stand on, not the substitute. Apostle Paul rebuked, saying that "you should be eating meat and yet you are still on milk." Meat is symbolic of sound doctrine and Biblical teachings. The early church grew by feasting on the Apostle's doctrine (Acts 2:42).

We should not just read feel-good, devotional material. We should also be studying the whole counsel of Scripture, the nature of God, and the history of our faith. This will give you solid grounding. Don't just read the Psalms and close your Bible. We should study the Epistles, read the Prophets, and analyze the Gospels. Ask God to give you a hunger for His Word. When Jesus spoke of eating His flesh and drinking His blood in John 6, He spoke of His teachings and words (John 6:63). We have an abundance of Bible study apps and features that were not available to our predecessors. We must use them if we want to sustain our fire for God.

Leaders, we must equip ourselves with the intellectual tools needed for this generation. This generation is one of fact checkers and investigators. That should never scare leaders because Jesus Christ IS the ultimate truth. Find out what's being taught in their schools and compare it with the Word of God. Rappers and pop stars are street philosophers. Find out what they are saying to society and compare that to God's Word too!

The Funeral Is Cancelled

Every great revival was preceded by serious challenges in the church. The Protestant Reformation, which revived the doctrine of salvation by grace, was preceded by great corruption, perversion, and greed in the church at the time. The Great Awakenings, which revived the belief in discipleship and sanctification, was preceded by complacency, worldly philosophy, and moral decline in society and the church. The Pentecostal Movement via Azusa, which revived the Baptism in the Holy Ghost and spiritual gifts, was preceded by serious racial bigotry through slavery, immorality, and a spiritual "coldness." The symptoms that we see today are signs that we are on our way to another great move of

God. Complacency is inevitable as we journey from "glory to glory," waiting for the coming of the Lord. As we move from one move of God to the next it is very likely that we can get stuck amidst the transition.

Thankfully, there is always another wave of glory awaiting us. God always has a remnant who has not bowed to Baal. And God always has the answer to the problems that plague our society. I do believe the intense battle between the generations is going to usher us into a powerful intergenerational revival. According to Malachi, intergenerational revival precedes the coming of the Lord. I believe, in my heart, that time is winding down, and this next move of God will come with the Lord turning the hearts of the fathers to their children and the hearts of the children to their fathers. This next great revival will bring us nearer to or into the return of the Lord Jesus Christ. The late Smith Wigglesworth once said that the next move of God after the charismatic revival (fulfilled in the 1960s-70s) will usher in the precious fruit of the earth and be the greatest revival ever seen in this world. Statistics and a quick read of the paper shows that we have not seen that revival yet, but it is coming. We must prepare ourselves for what God will do when the Bleeding Church is made whole and the Dying Church is raised up.

Epilogue: A Message to the Bleeding Church

As we prepare ourselves for what God will do, we must not become stuck in the monuments of the past. Don't build a monument on what should be a movement. We can't be so set on what was said that we ignore what the Spirit is *saying*. A good foundation is supposed to be built upon. A good foundation doesn't need more foundation, it needs to be *exceeded* and *advanced*. Much of what was seen in the yesteryears, even the erroneous things, were necessary to lay the groundwork but are not necessary for continual action. Hebrews 6:1 (KJV) says, "Therefore leaving the principles of the doctrine of Christ, let us go on unto perfection; not laying again the foundation of repentance from dead works, and of faith toward God." We should not be repeating the same things to the same people. We should be growing, expanding, and advancing the works of our Fathers.

Lastly, before you say, "This new generation don't know nothing about such and such," ask yourself, "Have I taught them anything about it?" Much of the problem is that we're assuming everyone should know everything, and we don't. Teach and impart into the next generation. Don't assume that they are all unteachable and sarcastic just because some of them are. There are many who are hungry for impartation and wisdom from those that have preceded us.

A Message to the Dying Church

First, to my fellow churchy, "old soul" millennials. Don't just seek the fathers, seek the *God* of the fathers. Many times, we imitate or desire what our predecessors did without finding out *why* they did it. The power is not in the action, but in the obedience to God. The power is not in the instruments, methods, or appearance and style. The power is in their submission to God and desire for Him above anything else. Research and find out why they did what they did. What prompted them to minister like this? What burden did they have for God's people that birthed this ministry? Then ask God to be with you as He was with them.

To all of my fellow millennials, It is important that we not desire to advance so much that we despise the foundation upon which we stand. Realize that the strong things we may say about the "old people" is the very thing that is holding us up. Many of them made sacrifices that we could never even imagine making, so that the church could see this day. The church does not expand in a vacuum, it is built on the foundation of the Apostles and Prophets. Anyone that claims to be building the Kingdom of God, but constantly tearing down their foundation may not be building God's Kingdom. Anyone that believes they are the first and only person to "get this thing right" is more than likely in error. Everything old isn't bad. Everything "new" isn't good and vice versa.

2 Thessalonians 2:15 (KJV) says, "Therefore, brethren, stand fast, and hold the traditions which ye have been taught, whether by word, or our epistle." Although the new things are cutting edge, only time will tell if they are lasting. Keep in mind that someday we will be

that old generation that we despised so much. We must honor them as we want to be honored.

As we love and honor one another, we prepare each other for the coming move of the Holy Spirit to receive His Bride. For truly, Jesus Christ is the same yesterday, today, and forevermore.

About the Author

Kesean (Kay-shawn) J. Joseph is a native of Brooklyn, New York. Kesean is the 3rd of 4 children born to Yvette and Kevin Joseph Sr. He was raised at the Institutional Church of God in Christ, International under his great Uncle, Bishop C.E. Williams Sr. He began singing solos for Bishop at the early age of two and soon began traveling with the church, the Institutional Radio Choir and on his own.

At the age of 8, his musical ability developed into preaching. At age 11, Kesean was licensed to preach as a "Junior Minister" under Bishop C.E. Williams Jr. The youngest to be licensed in his organization's history. He began ministering locally at youth services, revivals and conferences. He was licensed a Minister under his uncle, Bishop J.C. White and Bishop Williams Jr in the Church of God in Christ International.

Kesean graduated from SUNY Plattsburgh with a Bachelor's of Science in Public relations and legal studies. He completed a Communications internship program with the Congressional Black Caucus in Washington, DC with an internship in the U.S. House of Representatives. His abilities as a public relations and social media strategist led him to work with many businesses, churches and artists.

He was ordained an Elder in April 2017 under Bishop J.C. White and continued to travel regionally and nationally preaching the Gospel of Jesus Christ. Kesean possess a unique ability to translate complex Biblical concepts into practical truths that are relevant to all. This preaching and teaching ability was recognized in 2018 by the Eddy Awards when he was nominated "Young Minister of the Year" on Impact Television.

Kesean continues to function with God's favor in both the ministry and the marketplace. He is graduating from Church of God (Pentecostal) Theological Seminary with a Master's in Church Ministry and Leadership. He is an instructor of Old and New Testament

Analysis at Dominion Bible Institute complete with published textbooks. To all these things he simply says "It's all about Jesus."

www.ingramcontent.com/pod-product-compliance
Lightning Source LLC
Chambersburg PA
CBHW051408290426
44108CB00015B/2198